STECK-VAUGHN PAIR-IT BOOKS

Farm Animal Sounds

Written by G. L. Reed

STECK-VAUGHN
ELEMENTARY · SECONDARY · ADULT · LIBRARY
A Harcourt Company

www.steck-vaughn.com

A farm has many sounds.

Pigs oink.

Ducks quack.

Cows moo.

Chickens cluck.

Horses neigh.

Can you make animal sounds?